WHERE I DRY THE FLOWERS

WHERE I DRY THE FLOWERS

Poems by
OLLIE SCHMINKEY

Button Publishing Inc.
Minneapolis
2024

WHERE I DRY THE FLOWERS
POETRY
AUTHOR: Ollie Schminkey
COVER DESIGN: Zoe Norvell
AUTHOR PHOTOGRAPHY: Mel Nigro

ALL RIGHTS RESERVED
© 2024 by Ollie Schminkey

Published by Button Poetry
Minneapolis, MN 55418 | http://www.buttonpoetry.com

Manufactured in the United States of America
PRINT ISBN: 978-1-63834-092-8
EBOOK ISBN: 978-1-63834-104-8
AUDIOBOOK ISBN: 978-1-63834-103-1

First printing

Forgiveness is a strange thing. It can sometimes be easier to forgive our enemies than our friends. It can be hardest of all to forgive people we love. — Mr. Rogers

CONTENTS

1	it was the last day
2	if i knew it would happen
3	it was the year i stopped trying to stop chewing my nails
4	maybe being sad was the easy part
6	who holds the one who holds the dead?
7	my father
8	a life like that
9	flow//wolf
10	child of mud
12	everything is gorgeous but i am always stepping out of the shower already drenched in sweat
13	urn
14	in the moments when we had been alone
15	local transgender adult searches sky for proof that they have been loved adequately from beyond the grave
16	no one has ever said to me *i know he would be proud of you*
17	it is one week until the two year anniversary of my dad's death
18	of course, we were wrong
19	the months after my father's death, in 10 plaques
21	controversial opinion: in defense of speaking ill of the dead
23	prayer for the winter solstice
24	my heart lives in the crawl space just big enough for a body on the upper deck of a Jayco Jay hitch camper
25	my father
26	the deer stand
28	ars moriendi
29	a week ago
31	a love letter to staying
32	the door was already open
34	if you opened me up
35	in my dreams he always comes back to life
36	i'm sorry
37	animals named after other animals

38	my grandmother
40	they lied to me about heaven
42	if it was a *blessing in disguise*
43	i look so much like my father
44	we didn't always have a name
45	it was never enough
46	i was never promised joy
47	i make up new colors for grief
48	emit//time
49	guilt
51	things we did(n't) say
52	i think i have accidentally become an optimist
53	i buy my grief second hand at the Goodwill Pay by the Pound
55	another thing i loved is dead
56	the years after
59	we drink coffee by the lake
60	forgiveness
62	it is the winter of 2018 and my father is dying
63	yesterday, i took my dad to the cemetery
64	inheritance
65	daddy
66	last night the apartment across the street was on fire
67	it's not that i didn't want to believe in god
68	moor//room
69	Robert Frost would have been a camping gay
70	i will not die from my father's illness
71	you were once a boy
72	for my father on the five year anniversary of his death
74	do the dead love us back?
75	home
79	acknowledgements
81	about the author
83	author book recommendations

WHERE I DRY THE FLOWERS

IT WAS THE LAST DAY

or
it was a whisper ambling in the mouth, or
a bee grazing its way through the grass, or
the tacky plastic of a hospital bed, or

it was the smell in our nostrils, or
the way the sun stole the skin off our arms, or
the shrill of a violin strolling through the heat, or
my father just one slice away from being in a bag, or

it was my bra too tight against my ribs, or
my fingers clutching other fingers, or
the nurse's voice a saunter through the blood, or
the way there was no blood, and it felt wrong, or

it was the stack of forms crushed beneath our pens, or
the way the crematorium worker wasn't quite pretty, or
the way his hair nested in my fist, or
the repossession of his wheelchair, or

it was the banana peel i forgot in the car, or
some fast twitch on the steering wheel, or
hoping no one would recognize me in the Wal-Mart, or
fingering the stacks of 5 dollar DVDs, or

it was feeling all of the water in my blood for the first time, or
pretending to be a girl at the funeral, or
eating Bomb Pops next to his ashes, or
convincing myself i would be ready after all this time.

IF I KNEW IT WOULD HAPPEN

it would still happen.
my father holding hands
with a can of Miller Lite.
me, making eyes at a beetle
tumbling along a branch.
me, just a pile of notebooks and leaves,
holding funerals for the flies
trapped in the windowsill.

i think i have a crush on death.
what is an obituary but a note
passed between fingers underneath the desk during class?
what is grief but my heart thumping,
waiting to see if death writes me back?

IT WAS THE YEAR I STOPPED TRYING TO STOP CHEWING MY NAILS

i spent the year bit to the quick and bloody-cuticled
and alive despite everything.

it was the year we cried in the car,
sitting so still we could hear our breath
go all the way to the bottom of our lungs.

it was the year we were grateful.

it was the year we sang "The Joker" by Steve Miller Band
and rolled bandanas around our foreheads
and drank lukewarm beer under a sky
full of stars so bright they could've knocked our teeth out.

it was the year i returned to the woods
and twisted pine needles between my fingers
and ate a grilled cheese every other day
and drank the juice at the bottom of
half cup containers of coleslaw, and
i did nothing that year, absolutely nothing,
except be there, and watch
and watch and watch and watch,
until the smoke rose so high up the stars ate it
and there was nothing left for me to touch.

MAYBE BEING SAD WAS THE EASY PART

grief, a meal harmonic,
tuneful hum of the ashes in the bowl,
scrunched eyebrows and a palm curled around a shoulder.

when someone says *i'm sorry,*
you are not supposed to say
if you knew the whole thing, you wouldn't be.

you are supposed to say *thank you,*
like their apology is a gift, some pledge
of sorrow to wrap around the wrist of your dead—
i'm sorry is the salt of the soup,
pity-boiled grief, and you are supposed to be grateful,
for the thought, for the prayer,
for the *thoughts and prayers,*
as if it wasn't some borrowed thing carried
on the tongue off of a Hallmark card.

an acquaintance of your mother's presses a hand
to her chest, disturbing the perfume there,
a gesture of her *understanding,*
and she is standing so close you could sneeze
and some of the droplets would make it into her eyes
before she could get a chance to close them.

you're not.
sorry, that is.

sorry is a word for milk spilled on the table,
or 5 minutes late, or a misspelling—
no, this sanctioned and practiced flinch has nothing
to do with an apology and everything to do with being seen,
and you guess, you should be grateful anyone even wanted to be seen.
you could have filled a coffin with
whiskey bottles and called it his rightful body.

so no, you don't think *sorry* is the word for it.
you don't think there is a single word that could even
touch the teeth of it. not a word that could
eat a single flame.

WHO HOLDS THE ONE WHO HOLDS THE DEAD?

which girl is waiting on the other side of that door
with a warm cup of coffee in her hands?

love is both an entire room and only a palm on your back.
love coordinates the funeral potluck.
love breaks up sticks with her knees in the dark.
love puts more kindling on the fire.
love taste tests all of the food to make sure
no one put meat in the pasta salad.
love makes your moment about you.
love listens about the hair.
she cooks you meal after meal and brings you a fresh shirt
and peels pull tabs next to old men and
drinks beer neither of you would have bought
and sings "Born in the USA" and gets drunk with you
until you are both too sloshed to drive home,
but it doesn't matter,
because wherever you both are, there it is.

MY FATHER

— a contrapuntal

alive	dead
he walks through the trees the sun sifting through his beard	my dreams every night turn to spiders with his face. there is a campfire burning out, & me, the white dust of only ash in my hands.
here i am just a kid a father with his favorite child	in my sleep, standing next to his bed again— he doesn't look like a body about to burn to pieces
he looks so much like a dad here we are: birds flying a pulsing river a summer picnic & that smile— a mouth wide open, his child newly awakened wrapped around his neck like rosary beads clinging to his body	dead silence— no voice, only an echo not quite gone yet. the pills are down his throat, the morphine into his stomach, his body only for the disease, the wound on his back becomes filled with blood, & me, standing next to the body. grief has hands twisted tightening in prayer: the last breath like a final amen
i loved him before i learned of his body failing & i held him so trusting that my love is enough	i could speak the prayer a thousand ways— still, god will answer for only god never for the living

A LIFE LIKE THAT

growing up was uncles and cigarette butts and
mouths sucking sunflower seed shells and *faggot*—
my cousin Henry was gay, and it was all anyone could complain about.
every family camping trip, the men with their lips curled up
like they were about to spit, and the women saying
i don't care i just don't want to hear about it all the time.

when i finally came out to my dad, both of us drunk in a hotel room
halfway across the country, me just turned 19
and him just starting to die, the air thick with *bitch*,
him slurring through a tale of some girl
sucking his dick at a party—
me finally more angry than scared,
you know i like women, right?

and he just shrugged,
like *dyke* was no longer
the safety pin i had scratched into my ankles
sophomore year. he *shrugged*,
like i had never fantasized about my funeral
when i was supposed to be saying my prayers.

how dare he pretend he had loved me the whole time?

his acceptance, the betrayal of all my proof,
all my years of hoarding love in secret spaces:
a drawing in the crack between my dresser and the wall,
Hannah's number renamed "Brett" in my phone,
all my self-hatred— for nothing, for nothing.

FLOW//WOLF
— *a reverse palindrome*

flow

all the teeth dragged out of him,
life like a string pulled from his throat,
the spit on the pillow, the pus on the sheets,
feet, stomach, face, into the cremator,
the skin and fat sloughing off,
melting into liquid against the flame.

//

wolf

his chest bare like some moon to howl at,
how we tipped our chins and made
the night echo against the trees,
the leaves tossing in the wind,
a fire against the clouds.

CHILD OF MUD

child of the garden hose wash down,
child of mouth open river swimming,
child of good dirt,
child of burning and burnt—
once, i pulled a fleece sweater
straight from the dryer and the too-hot zipper
burned a scar in the hollow of
my throat like a welted honeycomb.

child of the northwoods,
child of forest and pulling fat gray wood ticks
the size of dimes from deep in the dog's coat.
once, when i was flicking the light switch
up and down, my mother told me it cost
ten cents every time i turned the lights on and off,
and of course, she just wanted me to stop being annoying,
but i spent the next year counting the expense of my sight,
almost a dollar to read a book before bed for a week,
twenty cents to pee in the middle of the night,
double if you also turn the bathroom light on,
and i became a creature who crept through the
darkness, and the darkness was always free.

child of the sweet smoke, of campfire
and the dank wet scent of weed on my father's coat.
child of venison steak and jerky, child of
animal to meat— once, i wanted to bring a deer leg
to show and tell, so my father sawed the leg off
just before the knee, and we wrapped it in a towel
in the freezer until Friday. i arrived, a third grade king,
swinging the knee joint open and closed like a switchblade,
clicking the hoof in the other children's faces—

child of precious dead things. of moths and walnuts
and mice. scab picker, collector of skins.
once, i ran too close to the fire and touched
my naked shin to the campfire grate and blistered
a burn the size of a golf ball, which i popped a week later
using my own fingernails, the pus like pine sap
running down my bare leg.

EVERYTHING IS GORGEOUS BUT I AM ALWAYS STEPPING OUT OF THE SHOWER ALREADY DRENCHED IN SWEAT

every day is a day he is dead.
the more i am alive the less i think of my life as a story
and the more i see it as just a bunch of stuff that happened.

his dead face, glasses dangling off an ear,
a trickle of spit, a stream in the woods, a frog crawling
out of my teeth, a eulogy that sounds like the hiss of a leaking tire,
and everything smells like a toilet full of old piss,
except when everything smells like donuts and leaves and french toast
and i am sad (but not) and i am making jokes people
don't laugh at but announce *that's funny—*

this time three years ago i touched a man who would
be a corpse in half a year, and i brushed his hair back
and watched *The Chew* every day in a bar
full of old men, and it is spring and each
of my teeth is its own little house with a door,
and i wonder who lives there,
and my partner and i watch queer people make out
on reality TV and plan what we want to have for lunch,
and today is a day, which means he is dead,
and he's dead and he's dead and i keep
his hair in a necklace and when people ask me what it is
i say *my dead dad's hair* and laugh so they don't
think i'm weird (i am) or sad (i am) and so they don't
have to feel sad (they should) or think about
their own death (they should) and sometimes
i can't help but think about when they slid him
in the cremator, his hair must have caught fire first:

his beard,
his eyelashes,
the patch on his knuckle i always rubbed when i held his hand.

URN

urn, noun: a vessel for storing

my skin is an urn.
a jam jar is an urn.
Lake Superior is an urn.

my mouth is an urn for my tongue.
a bed: an urn for our sleep.
a memory: an urn for that last breath.

IN THE MOMENTS WHEN WE HAD BEEN ALONE

a wet rose unfurling in his chest,
we could have said anything.
i could have asked anything i wanted.
we had time, we had so much time
but not enough—

the hands do what needs to be done—
a bandage, the dishes, a clean pair of underwear,
and so, i chose to say nothing every time.
each day was measured in tenths of a sandwich eaten,
four Cheerios, a tablespoon of milk—
but we never stopped pouring a full bowl.

we knew about death and it knew about us
and we blustered in the kitchen together,
the smell of an onion too strong,
the piss blooming against the gray of his sweatpants.

oh, how he hurt us and how we loved him
and how he was dying and we were watching
and counting pieces of cereal and writing
them into a chart scratched into an old notebook,
the numbers thawing down the page
where my mother had accidentally set a glass of water—

and so, we couldn't have said anything other than what we said,
about cows and deer and grouse and butterflies and
county maintenance, and my father never got good
at spelling, always w-h-e-a-t-h-e-r *weather*,
but i guess it was, the edema birthing out a
storm through the pores in his legs,
each pore a mouth opening in prayer,
a flood again— only this time,
god chose to save no one.

LOCAL TRANSGENDER ADULT SEARCHES SKY FOR PROOF THAT THEY HAVE BEEN LOVED ADEQUATELY FROM BEYOND THE GRAVE

no one has ever said to me
i know he would be proud of you.

NO ONE HAS EVER SAID TO ME
I KNOW HE WOULD BE PROUD OF YOU

too much flank.
too many tattoos.
too queer.
talked about it.
didn't.

as a boy, my father once trained a crow
to return nightly to the porch.

i try to train my memory the same way.
a host of beaked treasures:

a necklace,
a nickel,
a lock of silver hair.

IT IS ONE WEEK UNTIL THE TWO YEAR ANNIVERSARY OF MY DAD'S DEATH

a not-yet-old man slumped in a chair,

his head dangling from his neck like a spare house key.

the way i could memorialize that last week:
a hawk on the telephone line,
a spider in the dip of a raspberry,
the deer tracks deep in the new mud—

in one photo,
i'm alone, outside in the wheat field.
i'm smiling like the sun is the only good thing,
my eyes the same brownblack as the pill cutter.

i must have left him alone inside.
maybe he was sleeping and i had to steal this moment,
or maybe my sister had come over and it was her turn then
and i was just walking out to my car, to leave,
which was always both the easiest and the hardest part.

i don't think my dad is a ghost.
there's nothing for him to haunt.
everything was so overflowing in the end—
not just the pain and the catheter bag and the
morphine slipping out between the cracks of his lips, but us,
my hands underneath his back, the dog curled on the floor
by his feet, the summer and its red fruit—

i don't remember what i was like before.
except that once, he was in the hospital and i was 300 miles away
in a car racing south, and all i had in my stomach
was a jumble of peach pits,
the grief blooming there ground into little bits of petals,
and i smiled to my friends in the backseat next to me
and said *i'm fine, everything's fine,*
don't turn the car around.

OF COURSE, WE WERE WRONG

we didn't know that the last eight months of the last six years would drag his life out deep from within him, that last breath pinched between fingers and pulled out, slick with bile, like the popped balloon Sarah's dog choked on at her tenth birthday party. when i was young, i used to think if you swallowed a watermelon seed, a watermelon would grow inside you. my father had a beer belly so round and smooth i spent the entire summer imagining the fruit inside him, worrying one day it would grow so large it would split him down the middle. of course, i was wrong. of course, all of the splitting was much smaller than that, as we halved ourselves in the car ride up, as i chewed the skin around my cuticles, as i cut his pills in two. we were wrong, because we had been lied to. Patch Adams cracks a joke and Jack slips into the cold water beneath the Titanic, and every hero gets the last word, gets any last words— the truth? the body is gone far before the body is dead. my father's last words, buried somewhere in Wednesday, maybe *don't pour water down my fucking throat?* when i was young, i used to think Steve Miller Band's "Jet Airliner" was "Joe and the Rhino," and my sister and i would sing, one seatbelt across both of us in the passenger seat of my dad's black Ford pickup, *big old Joe and the Rhino, don't carry me too far away,* and i would picture the rhino, running and running with reckless abandon, and poor Joe (who was both Big and Old), holding on for dear life. and now, i go back, try to rewrite the lyrics of my father's last words— maybe, there was something else. maybe, later in the day, he told me he loved me.

THE MONTHS AFTER MY FATHER'S DEATH, IN 10 PLAGUES
　— *sonnets*

i. water turned to blood // ii. frogs // iii. lice

it is the thirtieth of August and
all of the water glasses hum with the
vibrations of the breath cutting his throat.
the coffee on our hands darkens as we
crowd around his skin. i send emails
and use words like *bereavement*, but when i
wipe at my cheek, my palm still comes away
smeared crimson with this debut miracle.
　// abundantly they came, wisps of his hair
　in my mixing bowl. nothing was itself
　ever again. my morning omelet, spliced
　with legs, the grief kicking my teeth to swim.
　　// my fingers scratching through little white flecks
　　of his burnt body: a father, a feast.

iv. flies // v. livestock // vi. boils

two weeks of the deer next to the pole barn,
flies swarm through its mouth like Tuesday's shotgun
in reverse. a firework of wings. his ash
in my room, my studio— his hair in
my car, orbed in glass, snow globe of my grief:
once, i tore the flight from a fly's back; now,
wings blizzard around my face while i sleep.
　// five months in but i still see the body
　fall behind my eyes: buckling legs, the quake,
　the meat of it. i still do not have a
　father. yesterday's butcher sends me a
　card. it's almost his birthday, after all.
　　// i imagine each fingerprint bubbling
　　up, rising through the skin like foaming yeast.

vii. hail // viii. locusts // ix. darkness

it is still winter although it is March.
i hate my friends so much more than i miss
him. they laugh and grief pebbles in my hands.
a penny, a golf ball— my grief cracks their
windshields, glass spidering until it bursts.
i shove shards into my pockets like old
photographs, his smile cut against my palms.
    // they ate the fingers off of all my friends,
    chewed off the corners of my dollar bills,
    gnawed their way straight through my front door until
    everything was a window to somewhere
    else— alone but the noise, good god, the noise.
        // birds thrashed their bodies against my windows.
        the sun fell into the mouth of the beast.

x. death of a firstborn

even the animals, God said. even
the sheep lost the first. even the locusts
and the flies. even the lice and the frogs
watched a face like theirs shrivel into dust.
the blood dripped from the doorframe of my love,
half a decade slaughtered for the wrong god.
my father, embered to the size of a
shoebox. i wonder if it would have been
so hard if this was not the first man who
had died in my hands, my first-dead, who crawled
back from this life into some other place.
either way, a mother weeps through the air.

it does not matter whose. god licks the tips
of his fingers: a dead father, a feast.

CONTROVERSIAL OPINION:
IN DEFENSE OF SPEAKING ILL OF THE DEAD
    — after E.J. Schoenborn

of course, at my father's funeral, i didn't.
my eulogy was not a mirror, but instead,
stories so close to lies they almost shared a kiss once—

in the eulogy, he is the dad who shows me how to change a tire.
i leave out the part where he drags me away from my homework,
six beers in, and forces me to torque and retorque the tire
until my arms are too sore to shoot at basketball practice the next day.

in the eulogy, we are no longer burying my father.
we are burying what could have been *a* father,
like the dusty print of a cardinal's dander on the glass
after it flies into the living room window.
from the outline on the glass, you can't see its broken neck.

he is both: the man who would make us
smoothies out of orange Kool-Aid and vanilla ice cream
and
the man who yelled when he drank and drank so often
i'd run to the basement and lock the door.

i refuse to euphemize him into a baseball-cap-wearing grill dad.
my dad wore a rolled up American flag bandana that he washed once a year,
soaked through with the summer's sweat. when the Kohl's cargo
shorts reached past his knees, he switched to making all of his
own shorts by cutting off his jeans, saying *they're not fucking called* **longs**.
my dad would blast his truck radio in the driveway, the doors flung open,
on weeknights until a neighbor called the house or the battery died—
when i remember him, i want to remember all of him.

so this is where we tell the truth. this is where we speak ill of the dead
when there is ill to be spoken. this is where an eye meets an eye,

a palm a palm, where the truth is no longer greased with
omission to slide more easily out of the throat—
a new eulogy, then:

this was *my* father; he died in my hands. i loved him,
like the god of the old testament, because i was too afraid not to.
and i loved him, because i knew i only had to do it for six months.
and i loved him, because he was my father.
and i loved him, because he needed me to.
and i loved him, like that first soft glow of sunrise.
and i loved him, like my own child.
and i loved him, god, i loved him so much
that at his funeral, i lied.

PRAYER FOR THE WINTER SOLSTICE

when i was young, my favorite time to run was at night,
out the unlocked front door swinging like a loose tooth,
legs slashing through the dark-dark of the country air.
there are a thousand ways to describe the stars:
my mother's freckles,
the dense bread crumb on fresh fried walleye,
river sand tossed up into the sky—

my wish for you on this longest night
is that the sky becomes all of your safest things.
my wish for you is that the dark is always a place of rest.
my wish for you is to sometimes feel the way you felt
before you ever knew danger,
when you flung the door open and you ran,
not away from or towards anything,
just to feel your good heart in your good chest.

MY HEART LIVES IN THE CRAWL SPACE JUST BIG ENOUGH FOR A BODY ON THE UPPER DECK OF A JAYCO JAY HITCH CAMPER

the beer cans scattered across the lawn like dead squirrels.
vodka with a full measuring cup as a shot glass.

i think, if we could have drained the alcohol
out of my father, he would have been so
empty that his skin would have shrunk like a raisin.

today, it was something bad that happened to me.
tomorrow, it was because something bad happened to him.
he is at once guilty and blameless.
he is at once punching a hole in my door
and a scared child at the foot of his own father's grave.

i take off my glasses and try to see the outline of the
way he loved me. he's dead and so maybe
he did see a rabbit and think of me.
he's dead and so maybe he *had* wanted to meet my first partner.
he's dead and so maybe he knew all along,
and i'm making the whole fucking thing up.

maybe we all held hands around the dinner table
while we prayed to a good god, over potatoes
crispy straight off the grill, while my dad and i
passed the barbecue sauce back and forth.

maybe i passed the salt to him and he took it and said *thank you*,
and we ate like life was the easiest thing that ever happened to us.

MY FATHER

— a contrapuntal

the hunter	the alcoholic
he never stopped	being drunk,
hunting for	his life's meaning
the final trophy	he reached for
his heart was	the handle of
a half empty cup	vodka
poured out	like the way
his blood pooled in	my hands
his body	reached for
the perfect cure	my father
didn't exist	before the bottle
the disease was	alcoholism
killing him	except we called it
cardiomyopathy	a broken heart
and still, in the end	he drank to the bottom
of his own death	every time
he dragged himself to	the bar,
the bottom of	rock bottom, addiction,
the hill	he would die on
at the end of	his own time. he drove up
the driveway	the road home
his half dead body	still drunk
leaned out of the window,	he never needed
a gun to kill	himself
a bullet	to stop
a heart—	only *we* did
witness that last breath,	once, he tried to give up the
endless bloody well of	thirst
the animal	that was his body
he killed because he wanted to	but he just couldn't quit.

THE DEER STAND

my father built his deer stand himself. think: Baba Yaga's hut but redneck, spindly pine legs holding up an entire room like the wobbling head of a tulip. the walls, plywood with fabric stapled over them like wallpaper. i imagine my father in the craft section of Wal-Mart, softly thumbing through each pattern until he found one with a dog that looked like his dog, a golden lab sitting in the reeds.

when i am old enough to remember but still young enough to complain the whole time, he shows me inside. we climb up the ladder he made out of 2 x 4s, his hand on my back so i don't fall. inside, the countertop is a piece of plywood resting on two overturned five gallon buckets. on the counter, there's a bottle to piss in, an eight by eight inch TV he powers with a chain of extension cords linked end to end the half mile back to the house, a pile of magazines he forgets have naked women in them and doesn't hide from me.

he's taken two of the old deck door screens and shucked the mesh from them, and has instead stretched the frames with cling wrap, creating these cellophane windows that he pokes the tip of his gun through, bragging about how he can still shoot but doesn't have to feel the wind.

when i am ten, he lines up beer cans in the yard for me to shoot with the .22. he wants me to be able to aim. when he is diagnosed, he gives my sister his BB gun with a grouse feather tied to it using an American flag bandana, so she can give it to her firstborn. he knows he will already be gone. when he dies, he gives me the title to one of the old Mustangs, the one with the mouse nest in the glovebox that he always intended to fix up, but never did. his whole life, he tries to give me gifts i don't want— but they're the only gifts he has.

despite this, i must admit, i am proud of my father, who built the house. i'm proud of my father, who invented a new way. i'm proud of my father's pride, and even of the animal he killed, and gutted with his own hands, and fed us with.

if you looked at a picture, you would see a white trash backwoods alcoholic nailgunning together pieces of plywood. you would see a small and dirty child flinching when asked to get another beer from the cooler. you would see the gun, i know you would.

but when i look through his old photographs, he's a boy, ordinary and smiling. when i walk through the woods, he's a man, a father, my father, who spends six hours out of every day sitting alone, drinking and watching an eight inch TV, listening for deer, and i know he feels it, i know he *knows*, and the only thing he can do is sit in the silence of it, and try to show me something good he's made.

ARS MORIENDI

— the art of dying, without fear or self-pity

i never saw my father scared. i only ever saw his teeth blooming
with vomit, his shins cratered with sores, and i wonder,
how many nights he pushed down his panic,
how often he reached out a hand to god,
all of his prayers whispered like the names of prescription drugs:
blessed be bumetanide. oh, holy morphine,
give unto me a window into death.

i know what there is to know about the body:
the fluids, the choke.
i know nothing about anything else.
my heart scrambles into my lungs
while i lay in bed and i imagine my father,
every night knowing he had no way of knowing
what was next, and i imagine our panic
as a string, reaching from the pulse under my tongue,
sneaking under the bedroom door, away and over and under
to wherever he is, or isn't, or i imagine him to be.

A WEEK AGO

— an erasure of "My Dad Died a Week Ago" first published in Dead Dad Jokes

       i search for a

                                        dead
                    feeling   ,

i reach out my arms and

i   go back   .
           i listen to the

                                                  flowers
          .

the wind on the back of my neck is
       soft   and it feels   like

           a new mouth,

i   smell the breeze and

  make   my father

                become

                        the summer   ,
        all i can do is
        walk into his

                                photograph,

                mouth   open   with laughter,
        and   exist.

A LOVE LETTER TO STAYING

i can't imagine being more than a quarter tank
of gas away from the place where my dad died.
i can't imagine packing up mugfuls of exes
and going some other place.
i never want to be some other place because
everyone i love is here. my home is a home is a girl
and a cat and everyone i love is in Minnesota
making pinky promises and running through the leaves
and eating and home is a place where we are eating together—

i see each one of our deaths stretched out in front of us
like a trail of breadcrumbs.
let's hold hands while we walk and let's pick berries
and eat them next to bikes and let's do everything
that makes us feel more alive and in love,
and before we go, we just *have to* have a garden,
and teach the cat to walk outside on a leash,
and see a waterfall an hour hike into the woods,
and ok sure, everything sucks—

but it will still suck regardless of whether we are making
syrup out of lilacs, so we should be eating flowers,
i think we should do it *tonight*, i think we should
make a fire in anything that can hold it,
because there's only like 3 ways to know if someone
really loves you, and they all happen sitting around a fire.

i ask my girlfriend *please tell me we can always stay here.*
and she say *yes, alright,* and i say *please never die,*
and she says *ok, you too,* and we pinch each other's butts
and drink the laughter straight from each other's tongues
and we are home and we are home and there is
nowhere else we'd rather be.

THE DOOR WAS ALREADY OPEN

we arrived, eyes still crowned with last night's drive,
and i wore the night before it like a hangover,
a headache just behind my eyes. i wanted to be there,
for the last of it, my father's lungs measuring the air
like so much stale flour, his throat grinding each breath,
and i was sure we would wake the neighbors.
of course, the neighbor was dying too, on the
other side of the wall, but i heard the thin laughter
of a wife or daughter, and i knew he wasn't dead
yet in the way my father already was.

my sister's husband was sent for coffee,
and my father died with the errand.
my sister's husband held out a palm for his change from
the gas station clerk and my father's life clattered to the floor,
and we parted the sheets like pulling the wings off a fly,
and the nurse unplugged the oxygen,
and my sister's husband returned,
a tray of warm drinks in his hand.

after that, i almost chickened out but didn't,
and asked the nurse for her scissors,
which were child sized and pulled out of a bib in her shirt.
i hacked the ponytail off of his head,
the same way they do when you are donating to Locks of Love,
although we weren't; we were keeping each strand
like silver wire, to wrap our grief in, to tie up our parcels home,
and i clutched it in my palm like one of the bouquets
we asked people not to send.

and then we signed paper after paper, and kept every single pen,
weighing them in our palms and mumbling
this is actually a pretty nice pen
sneaking six of them into my mother's purse,

and, despite ourselves, sipping at the coffees
that had killed my father.
but of course, they didn't kill him
any more than Thursday had killed him,
or August. but here we are, ten days away from the five year
anniversary of his death, which will be a Wednesday, and last
year it was a Tuesday and soon, soon,
he will have died on every single day of the week.

IF YOU OPENED ME UP

i think in the middle of me you would find
an old Jayco Jay truck bed camper, the kind that hooks on top
of a pickup truck, maybe a 1986 black Ford, just a guess,
a place to crawl into and feel safe parked among the pine cones
and scraggly grass. i think safety is a smell,
the pines drifting down towards a river,
a girl: the morning's coffee and chewing gum.

i never want to live a day without the marigold of a girl's mouth.
i always want to be in awe. the river on my ankles makes me
hug my grandmother, and i always tell myself i should leave.
that things that make me feel connected and grounded should be done
only in moderation, and i wonder, how i've gotten so far
but am only just now realizing that feeling good
doesn't make you a bad person.

confession: i have a Pinterest board of people who have
converted vans into tiny, gorgeous homes.

i think people love gemstones and astrology not because they're
vapid cliché douchebags but because nature is amazing and we
want to feel connected to something.

i wonder how i let myself get tricked into
believing that life isn't all about *living* here,
and feeling all kinds of ways when the sun licks your shoulders.
when was i taught that feeling good was something only
stupid shallow girls like, as if there was ever such a thing
as a stupid shallow girl, as if a shallow river wasn't always
the warmest and most beautiful place to be.

IN MY DREAMS HE ALWAYS COMES BACK TO LIFE

not in, like, a zombie or Jesus-y way.
he died, like in real life, but then somehow
it is months later and i am still listening
to the slosh as i pour the bedpan into the toilet.
it is months later and i'm walking in the woods
with my cousin, and i keep turning to him and saying
yeah, but isn't it weird that he died and now,
he's, like, alive again?

i have this dream over and over.
he dies, but he's still sick forever.
he dies, but he still needs me to clean the
old hair out of his hairbrush.
he dies, but he's still here, sort of,
always sleeping in a room with the door
cracked, always just upstairs,
the sound of his gasping clawing
out through the sliver of light.

I'M SORRY

i'm sorry, that in the end, i couldn't do more than i did. i'm sorry, for the way i let the decade leak out all its air, the party long over. i'm sorry, for the globes of laughter we strung above your dead body, but we had to make a light somehow, so we could see what you really looked like. i'm sorry, for my grief legless but still kicking my throat before you were even dead, premature creature, midnight rooster, how we screamed long before the dawn broke, and then broke us. i'm sorry, for my clammy palm, for sweating through your eulogy, for performing it just as much as i spoke it. i'm sorry, if the lament seemed waxed, if my main character lacked development, if the plot had too many holes and loose ends. i'm sorry, for the scaled scab on your back, from the time i couldn't catch you fast enough. i'm sorry, for the shreds of skin, for the blood like dew beading across your shoulders, and i'm sorry, too, for the bandage, for the clinging of adhesive, for the glue in the hair, for the pain we caused to heal the pain, for the too-tight braiding of hair, for the tears in the car still fogging my eyes when i walked in the house, for the med chart and the pictures of your sores, and i'm sorry for you, and i'm sorry, *i'm sorry,* but i'm also sorry for me, the way your death outlined my entire life, each day black-rimmed and flattened until we lost a whole dimension and were just sketches jerking in and out of the frame, and i'm sorry, that i only remember the parts i wrote down, all the gaslights blown out on the street, my memory snuffed out with the dawn's rising, because how, how, how, could you stare directly into a light like that.

ANIMALS NAMED AFTER OTHER ANIMALS
— a sonnet

what gift of taxonomy: *leopard moth,*
rhinoceros beetle, bat falcon; each
tardy creature named for an older beast.

the ancient animal christened before
my father: death. the IV cleaved into
his arm like the hyphen in a last name.
death-father. funeral-bed. cocoon-grave.
an urn is nothing if not chrysalis.
a body changed to a new body more
easily carried by the wind. i know,
dust to dust, ashes to ashes— the flames
devoured his hair first: what a smell his
metamorphosis must have made, the stench
of dying, of an animal reborn.

MY GRANDMOTHER

goddess of the canned peach,
who could slit a fish lengthwise
with one smooth motion.

my grandmother, who
promised me her sewing machine
if i promised i wouldn't cry when she died.

my grandmother, who
pan fried blueberry pancakes in hot oil,
who always said *fingers were made before forks*
and ate with her hands whenever she wanted.

my grandmother, who, on seeing my sister's bikini,
stripped down to her bra and rode around the
campground on her bike yelling
My bra covers more than your swimsuit does!
and laughing and laughing and laughing.

my grandmother,
who birthed half a dozen boys that voted red my entire life,
who stayed silent while they screamed Bible verses at my cousin,
who i hadn't seen in years because
after i came out, i just couldn't bring myself to come back.

but now i'm here.
and my grandmother, who can no longer remember who her son is,
my grandmother, who is only conscious for an hour at a time,
my grandmother, who is dying,
smiles like she isn't when she sees me,
and i am once again *hers*, and she grabs my hand on the couch,
and squeezes, and shakes it a little,
like she is trying to settle down the flour in a measuring cup,
and tells me that she loves me,

her eyes like the lake in her front yard,
her love floating up like a blanket of lily pads,

and she never says the word *gay*, but she does say
i made some mistakes with your cousin Henry.
she never says *gay*, but she does say *how is Natalie doing?*
she never says *gay*, but she does say *special* and *i missed you*
and *i want you to know i have always loved you.*

she is dying, quickly now, in that slow sudden way,
and any moment, i will get a call and cancel
some thing or another to go see her body,
burnt or unburnt, gentle, still—

when i was young, she told me not to cry for her
when she dies. i promised then that i wouldn't cry,
but i didn't know then who i would grow up to be,
and i didn't know then how much she would love me anyway.

THEY LIED TO ME ABOUT HEAVEN
— a sestina

when i was 10, we hiked to a lake at the high fall,
where my sister and i swam and sunbathed
on the big rocks that jutted out of the water. like heaven,
the sun was what i imagined a kiss would be like when i was older.
i would carry my tan skin around with me for months
into the winter, proof i had been loved.

on my rock, i was a prince, a king beloved
by his people. i had feasted on smoked white fish at the fall.
when i came back to land after minutes or months
i discovered dozens of black leeches had also bathed
on my throne, and in those seconds, i grew older,
my thighs dripping with bodies, a scream so loud heaven

could hear it, but of course, heaven
ignored me. fifteen leeches clung to my legs and loved
my blood senseless. i laid down on a picnic table older
than i was and waited for their bodies to fall.
my mother poured salt until they were bathed
and brined with sweat, and it took months

for the blisters of their mouths to fade, months
before i looked at water and again saw heaven.
my child legs, weeping and bathed
with blood. i could measure how much i had been loved
only by how much salt could fall
from my body. i grew new skin as i got older,

but every mouth grew bigger and older
too. in the end, they dragged the water out of my father for months—
his legs, weeping, the edema burst through his skin like a waterfall,
but there wasn't enough salt in heaven
or earth to brine the illness. so i loved
him throneless, kinged him instead with liquid morphine, bathed

in the clear-soft glow of the curtain-cracked sun, bathed
in dozens of shriveled years as he never got to grow older
than he was. we feasted on small talk, we loved
the weather, we swam in that blue-gray room for months,
the carpet peeling up at the edges like the lip of the shore, heaven
gnawing chunks off of him until the summer turned fall

and swallowed him, crowned him with flame. i loved him senseless, bathed
the still-orange fall forest in an early ash-snow, begged some older
future to pity me, to smoke-screen the months, to close that greedy mouth of
    heaven.

IF IT WAS A *BLESSING IN DISGUISE*

then the blessing's disguise was one of those
trench coats full of watches, except every
watch ticked with a memory of something
you wished you'd never have to have seen.
in this one, it's just past one and he's puking into the sink.
in this one, it's midnight and his breath barely slips out of his mouth.
in this one, it's 10 a.m., bright, and your sister's husband
has just left to get you all coffee, and you almost didn't come today,
because it was his first day in the hospice ward,
and you thought you might let him get settled in,
and you'd already taken off a lot of work,
but you came, because your sister called,
so you were there, for the most important moment of your life,
and the last one of his.

if it's true, that it's *better late than never,*
then you edged your toes right up to *never's* line,
played chicken with *never,* kissed *never's* lips
until you'd almost gone too far—
but no, you *were* there. and you were twenty-four
and he was six years into his diagnosis and you
would have let *never* choke you to death
for at least five and a half of those years, but it didn't.

and if it's true, that *when it rains it pours,* then
when a father dies, he dies a thousand small ways.
nobody cares if the tree in the forest makes a sound,
but he did, and you couldn't help but catalog each one,
each small jewel of pain, each whimper and gasping laugh,
until you had gathered every single last sound he
had in him, and he had no choice but to die in silence.

I LOOK SO MUCH LIKE MY FATHER

sometimes it feels like i watched myself die.

his tongue, blanched and lutefisked.
my tongue, a stone in the jaw.

sometimes i imagine grief as a ball of light,
the way you look into the sun and it makes your eyes water.

i think grief is always at least two things:
one, the constant realization that your expectations for the
future were wrong, and two, death has happened and it will again.

i come from people whose fathers grasped
the necks of their children like bouquets of roses.

my grief forgives his violence because of the violence before it,
the father of a father, the fist of a fist, the mouth of a mouth—
and did i mention his mouth?
how the corners were endless and caked with drying spit?
how we practiced loving each other like a song we
had never learned the words to?
how eventually, he died, and i saw my own eyes close
and knew that everything in the world had already happened.

WE DIDN'T ALWAYS HAVE A NAME

or we did, until the book was burned.
until someone's mother ripped a note in two,
our lineage torn from our hands
and stuffed to the bottom of the trash can.

i promise, there is no way of loving we could invent.
it has all been done before a thousand ways.
there is nothing more ancient than your lips
against mine in the CVS parking lot.

this love is older than any god
who would try to take it from us.

IT WAS NEVER ENOUGH

i had just barely begun to learn how to love him,
as his body shrank into the borrowed hospital bed.
everything was on loan those days, except my grudge,
which i clutched between my fingers like a bird in a cat's jaw.
i tried to love him like that, one finger curled around the throat
of my childhood and the rest around his neck.

then i started to know him. only in side conversations,
yes or no questions, the commercial breaks,
do you need some more morphine,
doesn't that egg salad they're making look like shit,
and somehow, in between all of that nothing grew something.

once, i laughed. genuinely, from my belly,
and a little bit of my anger flew up through my mouth—

once, towards those last days,
he was sitting on the couch blowing snot out of his
nose like a child, and i ran, with a tissue, to hold it
under his nose as he blew, to wipe his cheeks
and chin, and love was created there, somehow—
to be tender with a father who had never been tender,
to be quiet with a father who had never been quiet,
to kiss a forehead that had never been kissed.

and so, from around the dead bird of my hurt,
i had no choice but to unwrap my fingers one by one,
because i couldn't hold both my hurt and his hand.

I WAS NEVER PROMISED JOY

i am ankle deep in the river,
the sun a ragged shirt slipping itself over my head.

everyone's dads are dead, but grief can't catch me here:
there is nothing but the river and my feet
and the sun and being alive.

i was never promised this, you know.
the news flashed murders of people like me,
the headlines dripping across the TV screen.
the whole first three years after i came out,
i checked all the corners for knives.

every time i looked into a puddle i saw
my face bruised and broken-nosed—
never in the future i walked into was there joy,
leaves crunching underneath my bike tires.
never joy, only righteous anger,
like some absurd screw that held the edges
of our community together, like the only thing we
could ever hope to have in common was dripping down
our chins in bathroom stalls.

now, i'm grimy with laughter
and the warm bodies i've pressed against mine,
because i'm alive, because the sun
kisses the delicious joint of my elbow,
and girls do too, sometimes, girls who are alive
in spite of this lineage, and what a gift it is,
to be here, in the river, where the reflection
of the sunset looks nothing like blood.

I MAKE UP NEW COLORS FOR GRIEF

i wait for my period.
i wait for the train.
i wait for the water to boil.
i wait for my father to die.

i ink the water cinnamon.
the train, a celadon mouth.
the water, a cellophane lava.
his arms, goldenrod and amethyst,
the pores darkening as the blood coagulates.
his hair, silver to cement.
the sheets, white turning eggshell.

i make up new colors for grief:
nettle aster. he will never walk me down the aisle.
creek bottom moss. he will never speak my true name.
burnt blister. he will never love me any other way
than the way he has. *glass beaker. purified water. acetone.*
how many names for the color of tears: *resin, quartz,*
diamonds falling on his ashes.

EMIT//TIME
— *a reverse palindrome*

emit

the oxygen, a slow beep and huff,
a dead element in a dead man's mouth,
his hair curled underneath him like
a question mark.

//

time

the limbs sinking into a tired mattress,
the dog barking at the door,
his pores deepening until his skin
stands on his face as needles,
like the hands of a clock.

GUILT

a nap on the couch for fifteen minutes
meant he could become a body in the other room while i slept.
every friend's birthday was spent checking the clock
with a hand on my phone.
even after he died, i couldn't go for a walk, or take a bath, or
laugh at a stupid TV show without the guilt
burning up the back of my throat.
the alchemy of dying, joy transformed to shame at the first cough.

if a person could die without you if you leave,
leaving becomes a pill.
if a person could die while you're off eating cake,
the cake turns to mold in your mouth.

if a person you love could die while you are drinking
coffee in the back of a cafe with a girl,
could die while you buy yourself a muffin at the counter,
if he could die while you sing along and he gasps for breath,
you become convinced that your joy itself could kill him.
what is easier. to murder him for the sake of a laugh
or to stay sad for the sake of his life?

it's been three years.
it's been three years and i'm finally
trying to separate the gold from the guilt.

for once, i dunked my entire head underneath the water
while the lake rumbled and it was just me,
a splotch of sun splayed among the waves,
the wind against my cheeks and my hair drying upwards.

last summer, my partner and i drove three hours north to ride horses,
and we made a special mix CD where every song has the word *horse*

in it. my horse kept stopping to eat leaves
and walking so far off the path
that my head whacked into branches,
but i suddenly and completely loved this horse
so much i didn't dare steer it back—

i'm trying.

the bike path swarms with daisies, and the grasshoppers
leap out of the way of my bike tires, and i am
sun-filled even though this is the day my dad died three years ago,
and what wouldn't he want more than for me to blast
"Save a Horse, Ride a Cowboy" driving to a campground
he took me to every summer,
where little yellow wildflowers hum with bees
and we sneak in a bottle of Jack
and build a fire out of logs we stole from empty campsites,
and the point is, what's the point of watching someone die
if it doesn't make you learn how to be alive?

THINGS WE DID(N'T) SAY

— a contrapuntal

dad, you told me	i was wrong, but i still
never	should have waited
to kiss a girl,	to taste her like a
wicked bible verse	now-sweetened berry
that you picked	fresh from the garden,
out of my	bee-swarmed
teeth	flowering with want.
at the end of every	*girl* is a prayer turned
meal.	inside-out logic,
you never told me	god loved me too much
to stay	hidden. i should have kept
away from	my silence. prayers like
drugs,	smoke up to heaven. i needed
to study for	god's love. unworthy, life just a
class.	game of hiding and
hiding	i wanted
the shame	to absolve my guilt. now, i know
i can find	god himself
at the center of me,	all along
you were the one who	prayed i was different. god spoke,
told me	a promise:
i was	never
wrong	to love like i do.

I THINK I HAVE ACCIDENTALLY BECOME AN OPTIMIST

not in like a *Lululemon, LiveLaughLove* kind of way
but more in like a
joy is a serious force to be reckoned with kind of way.

my queerness has for too long been defined only by violence.
when i came out, each of my fingernails was a gravestone
for someone i could have loved if only they had been given the chance.

imagine, knowing you would be killed for your love and loving anyway.

i stare into the barrel of a gun and see two pinky fingers linked
underneath the plastic paneling of a wobbly diner table.
how many people have died so i can whisper to my girlfriend in the dark?
how many bodies have slipped themselves into my drink?
how many ghosts are rooting for my joy?

I BUY MY GRIEF SECOND HAND AT THE GOODWILL PAY BY THE POUND

in all of the pictures in the months before my grandmother went, she looks exactly like my father. it's hard to tell if it's the way their hair flickers out around their faces, or if the real family resemblance is just the nearness of death.

at her post-death family campout, all of my cousins and aunts and uncles sit around the fire talking about all of the health ailments that are killing or trying to kill them. Patrick slipped a disc in his back that paralyzed him from the neck down for a week and now he runs a business making gummies out of weed because that's the only thing that helps with the pain, and he passes the gummies around the circle until half of the fire is high off their fucking minds, and we hardly talk about my grandmother at all, the one who is fresh-gone, her name still soft in my cheek.

except me and my cousin Henry instantly form a gay corner, and we bow our heads together and whisper about how much our grandmother loved us, despite and because of who we were, ahead of her time, and my grandmother, who birthed my father, who died, is dead, and i am once again holding out an urn, begging for some salt to keep and put on my mantle— and i drove to the edge of the wilderness, where the lakes blink open like hundreds of eyes, up 38 and onto a dirt road, and bless a dirt road, my flat tire, the slow way home, bless that my grandmother went from nothing but being old, although the world wrapped too many fingers around her neck in her sleep, bless that for once, she is the buried and not the burying, the eulogized and not the eulogizing, bless her silence, bless the wolf spiders the size of quarters dotting our tents in the yard, bless the entire *nineteen* dogs swarming around our chairs, even the dog who peed on my tent and keeps trying to hump my mother's papillon, bless the porta potty in the driveway; so many of us love my grandmother that we have created a pile of shit so large my aunt dubs it "Mount Poo-ji," and bless my cousin Patrick, who gives me something i never thought i'd get: an apology.

and just like that, my uncles ask about my partner, and i walk down to the lake to put my feet in and feel sad, and i search for frogs in the lily pads but don't find any, and then my cousin's kid, who is old enough to be my cousin, comes down with one of the nineteen dogs and we laugh about something and i put my socks back on, and everyone goes to sleep in their tents and campers staked and parked in the yard, and we wake up to a world that knows us more than it did the night before, but still feels less somehow.

ANOTHER THING I LOVED IS DEAD

most days, i know my place.
most days, i see the veins inside of a leaf
or the branches of a river
or the sweat of rain on a window
and i am slick with geography—
the world and i slide over each other
like the soft film inside of an eggshell,
and even if i don't *understand*, i understand:
i am part of this thing, we are the same.

the tendril of green that splits open the acorn shell.
my heart is growing a tree, i guess,
and it makes me forget myself.
another thing i loved is dead,
and another, and another,
their bodies piled up like leaves in my throat.

THE YEARS AFTER
— an erasure

I. year one

i break my fingers into my coffee every morning.
i write half a novel about my own dystopian future,
vow to complete it by year's end. i never finish a bite.
we could keep digging this hole until the end of time.
every day limps to the table like a bad promise. i gnash until sleep.
i find that every animal is an omen from my father's ghost.
i thought my heart was ready.
joy whimpers at the foot of the bed.
my grief doesn't call anyone back.
my tea steeps until i gag with the strength.
i am not ready to move on. i drink my water
through my clenched teeth.
i know i could be happy, but i still can't imagine the day.
i make a pinky promise to my grief, a blood pact,
myself and the grief trading baseball cards
and bubblegum our whole lives—
i wait for the sun to set like a falling star,
so we can go in search of the dusk
in my never ending river of grief, to wrap our fingers around
the frogs we find in my chest by their throat songs,
until the world sleeps and from that sleep, wakes up,
and i can hear the crickets warbling like a cruel laugh,
and i am never alone again.

II. year two

```
i break
                        my own
vow              by year's end. i never
     could keep
                        a    promise. i          sleep.
i find                             my father's ghost
         my heart     ready
             at the foot of the bed.
my grief
       steeps until i
  am    ready to        drink

        i could           still
   make a      promise to my      blood     ,
myself and the grief trading
               our       lives—
i wait for the           falling star
                    of
    my                 grief  to wrap    fingers around
                   my              throat
until the world                  wakes up,
and i can hear              a cruel laugh,
and i am      alone again.
```

III. year three

i break

                                                            my father's
               heart

                  i
am   ready to

    make a   promise to
myself

        the   star
                  of

            my   throat
                            wakes up,
and i can   laugh
              again.

WE DRINK COFFEE BY THE LAKE
— a sonnet

i cry while we drink coffee by the lake.
he will die in three days, and i feel it.
it's been four years, but my body still knows.
this year he will be dead for half of the
time i've spent loving the love of my life.
the longer i love her, the larger the
greedy percentage. at ten years of love,
his death will be almost two thirds of it.
you could eat a meal this way, or maybe
learn to forgive someone. eventually,
the years i loved her while he was alive
at the same time will be just a sliver,
a crack in the door of my life, an eye
barely closing or opening from sleep.

FORGIVENESS

i never said it out loud.
maybe my father wanted forgiveness
as much as i wanted an apology,
but we stayed silent,
the grudge smooth as a pearl
underneath our tongues.

but it doesn't mean i didn't.
forgive him.
and it doesn't mean he wasn't sorry,
the last bit of his life pinched
between the fingers like a kerchief,
or a white flag.

i was there, wasn't i?

and he never asked about a boy again,
not during those last days.
we had sanded our hurt down to the bare wood,
and we pretended at love with our best effort,
trembling the whole first week i brushed his hair,
until maybe we had gotten it, at the end.

he invited my partner camping.
he would die before, but still.

it was not the 3-part apology
meme-shared on Facebook circa 2013.
it was not an atonement.
there was no action plan for restorative accountability.

instead, we both agreed, silently,
that we would pretend he had always accepted me,
and in return, he would die.

we struck this bargain without realizing it,
my hands deep in the rattle of sorting his pills.
we decided it over dice poker, the tips
of his fingers already purpling.
we made a pact while i took off and put on his socks,
while i rebandaged his sores,
while i cooked him grilled cheese like a mother
and tucked him into bed.

i kissed him on his forehead every night—
what more forgiveness could he have possibly asked for?

i was there, shuffling inches behind his
every step in case he fell,
washing the puke bucket in the sink,
rubbing lotion on his feet.

when he offered me his death as an apology,
i took it.
of course,
i took it.

IT IS THE WINTER OF 2018 AND MY FATHER IS DYING

when i am eight, our dog dies in the hallway.
it's winter, it's always winter,
so the ground is too frozen to bury her.
my father puts her in the sled in the yard
and we visit her body for weeks,
running our hands through her frozen fur,
hugging her corpse, saying her name as a puff of
white steam into the air.

even my father knows she can't stay there in the
sled being dead and getting petted until spring.
the river isn't quite frozen over, so he loads her
into the back of his pickup and drives her down.

a few days later, Neighbor Bill calls—
i'm so sorry, but i think your dog died.
i found her washed up on the bank by my fishing hole.

and so my father once again puts her in the back of the pickup,
this time with her feet cinderblocked, and drives her down.

//

my father is a man who can never stay dead.
his hair keeps washing up on the shore of my dreams.
i run my fingers through his ashes and they are soft as fur.
how many times we have driven him down,
little bits of bone puffed white into the air, and we know—

to love someone is to eventually throw them into a river,
again and again, to swallow a corpse and then drag it back up the throat.

now, it is winter, always winter,
and we walk down, where an alive man with an alive dog
tells us to look at the reflection of the trees in the river,
the river so still it looks like a lake,
the river so still you could never guess at all the bodies underneath.

YESTERDAY, I TOOK MY DAD TO THE CEMETERY

we walked among the graves and made jokes:
these people's last name is Porn;
this singing angel looks like it's about to suck a dick—
but mostly we smiled down at everyone,
especially Gerald and Regina Porn
(who must have had a tough time as the
clearly very religious people that they were),
and we loved them all equally and a little extra,
just in case the cold had kept their alive ones away.

sometimes i imagine the snow as the ash of our dead,
who got too lonely under the ground and inside of jars,
so they came outside to go sledding,
to feel our good cold breath,
to sneak into the house on the fringe of a boot,
to be held in the hands
as we make bodies out of them again.

INHERITANCE

i.
i come from a family of loud laughers. as a kid, i could find my mom across the Wal-Mart by the sound of her, echoing through the bra aisle and past the frozen shrimp.

ii.
i know, everyone must die, but i come from a family of people who die and who die young, who die from hearts and lungs and cancers and pills and their own brains. they die from so many things i mix up the names, who had leukemia and who had diabetes, who was cancer and who was embolism, who survived the stroke and who called in the hearse.

iii.
sometimes i press a fingertip to the dip underneath my jaw and feel my heartbeat. every so often it stutters and i imagine the dance the blood does inside my chest. there is a special kind of fear of knowing you might die from something you watched kill someone you love. i go to the doctor and get my cholesterol checked. i wrangle my torso through situps so that i can choose what i can of my inheritance. i grasp the tilt of my cheekbones, the fuzz of an eyebrow, the way i pronounce the *o* in *love*. at the doctor, i barely leave a box unchecked. *family medical history* is a stack of photocopied coffins down the side of the page. at family gatherings, you have to hug every single person goodbye. the rounds can take a full half hour, and i think about this, this inefficiency of love, the time we spend spending time with each other, the parade we make through the ICU halls.

DADDY

— a sonnet

all hail the baseball cap, the button up,
the pun, the wrench, the dirt under the nails,
the dykes oiling the chains of bicycles.
all hail the pickup truck bed full of queers
driving down a dirt road to the river,
the dust kicking up behind us like the
opposite of a eulogy. all of
our fathers are either shitty or dead
(or shitty *and* dead), so we make it new:
daddy, but good this time, skip the violence,
keep the backyard garden, fresh strawberries,
the porch swing, the musk of a shed, catching
a bug to bring it outside. bless how we
became everything we ever needed.

LAST NIGHT THE APARTMENT ACROSS THE STREET WAS ON FIRE

and we watched from our sunroom as
two firemen pulled a bundle from the smoke
and laid it on a stretcher,
the door like a mouth exhaling a long drag from a cigarette—

that's how it happened, the articles say.
a cigarette not quite put out, a living room carpet.
they tell me he died, this man, and his cat.

today grief makes my bed even though it has no right,
this stranger, who i only ever saw in a glance,
a mass of limp limbs shrouded by the dark of December,
but grief is not a stranger to me,
and no matter what i do,
something inside of me answers.

if there's anything my own grief has ever wanted,
it's for people to love my dead,
even if they have no right to it.
so i'll say it:

i saw you, and i loved you as much as i could
in the ten seconds between the door and the ambulance.
i saw you, and i sent up a prayer for you,
even though i'm not the praying type,
just in case you were.

IT'S NOT THAT I DIDN'T WANT TO BELIEVE IN GOD

i drive to a gay pride festival in my hometown
and twirl my girlfriend in front of truckers and
construction workers and farmers with their sleeves ripped off,
and we are forty people sitting in a park long enough
to be seen by anyone who wanted,
and i can't stop crying at everything:

the look people give me when i say i grew up here,
the girl and my friends and the women with short haircuts—
the place i had my first art show is screening
LGBTQ movies until 9 p.m., and i can't ever
possibly explain it:
the hurt, the hunger, scratching at the label
on my shorts, being in love, here, here, *here*—
the place god was my first love,
and then god was the worst breakup of my existence,
and god was buying a gun at Wal-Mart,
and god was chewing tobacco and playing Nickelback,
and god was saying *crik* instead of *creek*
and spitting out the window of his truck
as he snaked a grease-gray finger under the hem of my skirt,

and my god, what a decade it's been.
my god, what a way to come home.

MOOR//ROOM
— *a reverse palindrome*

moor

the men all raise their guns
and the grouse trip into the sky.
my father always taught me to
listen for the grouse, like a drumbeat,
like a heart beating faster and faster
until it explodes.

//

room

we all raise our hands
and our prayers trip into our teeth.
the disease taught me most how to listen.
the heart, a drumbeat.
the heart, beating slower and slower
until it becomes the sky.

ROBERT FROST WOULD HAVE BEEN A CAMPING GAY

the sunset is a feral orange,
the berries puckered against the treeline
like our fresh-picked acne scabs—
if nature was anything, they'd have to be trans.
how many times have we all lost ourselves
in the woods and emerged as
someone worthy of a new name?

all hail the camping gays.
the salty pink of our corneas
as we blink through the fall wind.
all hail the dildo stashed in the glovebox like a gun.
the teeming black of the asphalt
as we rush towards a clean lake,
the waves drinking our bodies up
like a body of water is in fact a body,
a queer body, hungry for our touch.

i'm in love with all the trees and i think they love me back.
i think a river is the gayest shit ever.
the frogs cheer me on from the banks.
smoke from the fire is a deep translucent blessing,
reminding me that we deserve to be here too,
we deserve to be here too, *we deserve to be here too*—
we deserve to laugh, flinging ourselves into water.
we are not just built for shame
and fear and waiting our turn.
this world is ours, too,
and if god did not make us in his image,
we'll just have to make god in ours.

I WILL NOT DIE FROM MY FATHER'S ILLNESS

a heart is a heart but a bottle is a bottle.
we can't say for sure it was the drink, but
you can only hold a thing underwater so many times
before it drowns.

i always thought it would have been the liver,
scarred like the meat of his left palm.
but no, the heart, then.

half a bottle of wine sits in my fridge until it turns,
and i remember every night before,
and there is nothing that can be taken from me
that i'm willing to give.

YOU WERE ONCE A BOY

standing in the doorway,
beams of soft light outlining your shoulders,
watching your mom get choked until she went limp.

i was once a child,
dragging my favorite stuffed animal to the basement,
your knuckles still splintered with my bedroom door.
an accident, really.
it doesn't sound like progress
unless i flip through the whole photo album.

it is, in fact, a gift— to come from such violence
and choose to be less of it.

i see you, at twenty, shipped off with the army,
your own father dead and buried
before you could return for the still-warm corpse.
i see you, barely a grown man,
fingers pressed to the window of an empty funeral parlor,
army fatigues sagging off your shoulders.

you had your first drink when you were eleven. *eleven.*

how could the bottle not become a father?
how could the bar not become a type of church?
how could a man find healing except in these places of worship,
where trauma sold for a dollar ninety-five
and every man there had seen a dead body?

even if you were gone, i knew where to find you,
to drive the loop between the TimeOut, the Cricket, the Legion,
search for your van with the back windshield
busted out and saran-wrapped over.

i can say it now:
thank you, for doing the best you could.

FOR MY FATHER ON THE FIVE YEAR ANNIVERSARY OF HIS DEATH

god, dad, you've been dead for five years and I'm not even thirty.
in your honor, today i cried in the car to Reba McEntire's "Fancy"
and left the windows rolled down until i passed Forest Lake,
the wind so loud i had to turn the music up,
the wind so strong i couldn't help but speed
and laugh when the song was over and feel what i'm sure
you always felt speeding with the music loud and the windows down.

dad, i could have been a sheet billowing on the clothesline.
i could have been a child drinking a root beer for the first time.
i could have been driving up to see you, and you could have been
taking me out to lunch at the Legion, and we could have been
pointing out the cows grazing on Northern Road
just before it turns to asphalt.

//

i spent the drive imagining the empty chair we would
have for you at our wedding.

//

today we discovered the plum trees. we were already making
crumble out of the apples from the trees you planted—
did you know they've fruited every year since you've died?
small, tart apples that fit in the palm of my hand
like eggs in a bird's nest.
we walked down the hill to check on the raspberries,
and we found the plum trees bending with these beautiful
perfect little plums, the size of grapes, impossibly sweet.

//

i am only now learning what it means
to plant something for someone you love
that will only bloom after you are gone.

//

i am not going to say anything about the alcoholism
or the yelling or the absence or the fear.
i'm not going to say anything about the morphine
or the last breath or the funeral.
this time, what i want to say
is that i spent the morning looking through photos of you—
your arms clutching your new puppy
while tears run down your cheeks—
listening to the five voicemails i managed to save
off of a cellphone that has long since stopped working.

in one, you start— *hey, kiddo, it's your old man—*
although you weren't old, not really, maybe fifty-two,
but you *were* mine, then, and you called to tell
me you had found me a new used car
after a teenager ran a stop sign and totaled mine,
and i imagined you in a stranger's driveway,
flashlight balanced between your teeth, peering under the hood,
checking the fluids and running a thumb over the battery's plugs.

i don't think i knew it then, but i know it now, today,
how much you loved me. maybe, if you were still alive,
we could have learned how to be friends. maybe,
if you were still alive, we could have driven up north
to Two Harbors to buy a smoked white fish and hike
to the falls, and the whole way up, we could blast
the music and feel the wind lift us up through our laughing mouths
like kites shrieking through the summer sky.

DO THE DEAD LOVE US BACK?

trapped inside an orb, an urn,
a photograph. how hard i had worked
before not to love him, to see only the drink
and the fist and the walls shaking.
to see only the man and not the boy he grew from,
only the yell and never the song.

i have learned to hope in the past tense.
to reach back through time and edit the memories.
a bigger smile here, the fear just a smudge on
the window, to build us a life where love
was easy and sure, not some dark hotel room
where my heart woke up the man next door.

and the dead are loyal once they are inside
the urn. once they are small and sinless. once
the fight has run out and they no longer have fists.

let this be where i dry the flowers.
where i keep his name tucked inside of my cheek.
where i honor the body, in all of its dust
and crumbling, and hold it like a match about to light.

HOME

my father left like a long Minnesota goodbye.
his death, shoes on in the entryway,
being shoved tupperwares of leftovers.

home is the place where you stay.
my sister bought a house 15 minutes from our childhood house,
and even though i've left, i've stayed.

last week, one of my client's dogs died
and i cried in the car on the way to Target.
even though i only saw her twice a month
for a couple of hours, i loved her long enough
to watch her die, which is the best case scenario.

sometimes i feel like i am a tree standing in the woods,
in one of those time lapse videos, while everything around me falls.

whenever i watch TV, everyone looks very old.

at my grandmother's funeral Labor Day campout,
everyone spends hours around the campfire
holding their cancers up to the light,
but then the next minute we are all laughing.

no one plans who will bring what, but there's
always plenty of food.
home is a place where everyone already
knows what to do, where grief and laughter
are like whiskey and ginger,
where the smoke clings to your clothes
and anyone who says that campfire smoke "stinks"
is told to shut the fuck up or leave.

if everything has to happen, i want it
to happen here, in between the endless lakes

and my mother's smile.
where you're never more than half an hour
away from a dirt road or a really good piece of cheese.
before he died, i told him that i loved him,
and meant it.

button poetry

ACKNOWLEDGEMENTS

First things first, a special thank you to *Frontier Poetry* for giving the poem "My Father" its first home, and to *Contemporary Verse 2* for "Child of Mud," "Flow//Wolf," and "If It Was a Blessing in Disguise."

Second things second (because that's how counting works), a big thank you to my folks at Well-Placed Commas— so many of the first drafts of these poems were written in community with you, and I am constantly inspired by the work and belonging we create together.

A big thank you to my early editors: Tyler and Zach— this book wouldn't be what it is without you! Thank you for all of your feedback, and sorry for anything I ignored.

Thank you to Allison and Strike Theater for always giving my poems and events a home— when I think about chosen family, I think about the spaces we make here.

Thank you to Button, for being the Best Ever. I feel constantly supported, cherished, and celebrated by you. Special thanks to TaneshaNicole and Patrick for being amazing to work with.

A huge thank you to everyone who read my first book, *Dead Dad Jokes*, to everyone who follows me on social media, to everyone who sends me incredibly nice messages— you all have helped me to feel way less alone in my experiences. Thank you for supporting my work, and most importantly, for seeing me.

As always, thank you to queer and trans people. I've often said that being queer has saved my life, and I think it's true. You have taught me so much not only about how to survive, but how to thrive. Every good joke I have, I learned from you.

Thank you to my mom and sister Leah— I know it is not always easy having a writer in the family! I love the time we spend together, and I love you! I'm so glad I get to call you my family.

Thank you to my dear partner Natalie, for being the first (and last) editor, for the countless hours of rearranging poems on the floor, for coming to all of my events, for holding my hand when I am sad, and for reminding me I shouldn't shit talk too much in poems I am publishing. I love the life we have created together— it is so much better than anything I could have imagined for myself. You are my favorite one.

ABOUT THE AUTHOR

Ollie Schminkey is a non-binary transgender poet and artist living in St. Paul, MN. They have spent the past decade coaching, mentoring, teaching classes, and running workshops for poets. They are the author of three chapbooks, as well as the full-length collection *Dead Dad Jokes* (Button Poetry, 2021) which was shortlisted for both the Midwest Independent Publishers Association and the Eric Hoffer Grand Prize. Their work has been featured everywhere from THEM to Upworthy, and they've performed poems in 19 states, with their work garnering over 3 million views on YouTube. When they're not writing and performing poetry, they spend their time making creepy+cute pottery under the name Sick Kitty Ceramics. You can find them touring nationally, making music, or playing with their cat Pete, who is always trying to eat things he shouldn't.

To take a class or to see more of their work, check out ollieschminkey.com.

AUTHOR BOOK RECOMMENDATIONS

The Only Worlds We Know by Michael Lee

This book takes us through addiction, grief, and loss with a sharp eye and ever sharper lyric. Michael Lee writes poems with images that are crisp like that first breath of winter. I could quote a line from every poem, but I'll leave you with this: "the dead are just barely beyond / what you can touch / and every life you could have had sings."

The Crown Ain't Worth Much by Hanif Willis Abdurraqib

This book is, simply put, incredibly good. Hanif flawlessly weaves narrative with intense, fresh images, and I don't overstate when I say this is one of the best books I've ever read. Some people write to try to change the world, and then there are others, like Hanif, who do.

Ephemera by Sierra DeMulder

Sierra's *Ephemera* is like a hug from your best friend after a long cry on the couch. This collection so tenderly holds both the grief and the joy of being alive, and each poem leaves you feeling in love with and so grateful for it all.

OTHER BOOKS BY BUTTON POETRY

If you enjoyed this book, please consider checking out some of our others, below. Readers like you allow us to keep broadcasting and publishing. Thank you!

Adam Falkner, *The Willies*
George Abraham, *Birthright*
Omar Holmon, *We Were All Someone Else Yesterday*
Rachel Wiley, *Fat Girl Finishing School*
Bianca Phipps, *crown noble*
Natasha T. Miller, *Butcher*
Kevin Kantor, *Please Come Off-Book*
Ollie Schminkey, *Dead Dad Jokes*
Reagan Myers, *Afterwards*
L.E. Bowman, *What I Learned From the Trees*
Patrick Roche, *A Socially Acceptable Breakdown*
Rachel Wiley, *Revenge Body*
Ebony Stewart, *BloodFresh*
Ebony Stewart, *Home.Girl.Hood.*
Kyle Tran Mhyre, *Not A Lot of Reasons to Sing, but Enough*
Steven Willis, *A Peculiar People*
Topaz Winters, *So, Stranger*
Darius Simpson, *Never Catch Me*
Blythe Baird, *Sweet, Young, & Worried*
Siaara Freeman, *Urbanshee*
Robert Wood Lynn, *How to Maintain Eye Contact*
Junious 'Jay' Ward, *Composition*
Usman Hameedi, *Staying Right Here*
Sean Patrick Mulroy, *Hated for the Gods*
Sierra DeMulder, *Ephemera*
Taylor Mali, *Poetry By Chance*
Matt Coonan, *Toy Gun*
Matt Mason, *Rock Stars*
Miya Coleman, *Cottonmouth*
Ty Chapman, *Tartarus*
Lara Coley, *ex traction*
DeShara Suggs-Joe, *If My Flowers Bloom*
Edythe Rodriguez, *We, the Spirits*
Available at buttonpoetry.com/shop and more!

BUTTON POETRY BEST SELLERS

Neil Hilborn, *Our Numbered Days*
Hanif Abdurraqib, *The Crown Ain't Worth Much*
Olivia Gatwood, *New American Best Friend*
Sabrina Benaim, *Depression & Other Magic Tricks*
Melissa Lozada-Oliva, *peluda*
Rudy Francisco, *Helium*
Rachel Wiley, *Nothing Is Okay*
Neil Hilborn, *The Future*
Phil Kaye, *Date & Time*
Andrea Gibson, *Lord of the Butterflies*
Blythe Baird, *If My Body Could Speak*
Rudy Francisco, *I'll Fly Away*
Andrea Gibson, *You Better Be Lightning*
Rudy Francisco, *Excuse Me As I Kiss The Sky*
Available at buttonpoetry.com/shop and more!

FORTHCOMING BOOKS BY BUTTON POETRY

Topaz Winters, *Portrait of my Body as a Crime I'm Still Committing, Special Edition*
Zach Goldberg, *I'd Rather Be Destroyed*
Eric Sirota, *The Rent EATS First*
Neil Hilborn, *About Time*
Phil SaintDenisSanchez, *self-portrait before & after my body*

Available at buttonpoetry.com/shop and more!